BUZZ BEAMER'S RADICAL SPORTS!

BY BILL HINDS

A Sports Illustrated For Kids Book

SPORTS ILLUSTRATED FOR KIDS is a trademark of THE TIME INC. MAGAZINE COMPANY

SPORTS ILLUSTRATED FOR KIDS Books is a joint imprint of Little, Brown and Company and Warner Juvenile Books.

Printed in the United States of America

First Printing: September 1990
10 9 8 7 6 5 4 3 2 1

Published simultaneously in Canada by Little, Brown & Company (Canada) Limited

Library of Congress Cataloging-in-Publication Data

Hinds, Bill, date.
  Buzz Beamer's radical sports/written and illustrated by Bill Hinds.
      p. cm.
  ''A sports illustrated for kids book.''
  Summary: Buzz Beamer, a real radical dude, introduces some wacky ideas for improving sports.
  ISBN 0-316-36448-7
  1. Sports—Juvenile humor. 2. American wit and humor.
[1. Sports—Wit and humor. 2. Wit and humor. 3. Cartoons and comics.] I. Title. II. Title: Radical sports.
PN6727.H5B88 1990
741,5'973—dc20
[Fic]
                                            90-33606
                                              CIP
                                               AC

HI, DUDES AND DUDETTES. I'M BUZZ BEAMER, AND I'M STANDING NEXT TO A STATUE OF DR. JAMES NAISMITH. THIS GUY WAS A GENIUS.

DR. JAMES A. NAISMITH
..FATHER OF BASKETBALL

ONE RAINY DAY IN THE 1890S, DR. NAISMITH NAILED UP A COUPLE OF PEACH BASKETS IN A YMCA GYM...

AND CREATED BASKETBALL.

HE'S THE ONLY DUDE I EVER HEARD OF WHO CREATED A SPORT.

WELL, TODAY I'M GOING TO SHOW YOU WHAT A SMART GUY I AM BY **RE**-CREATING A FEW SPORTS. I'M GOING TO ADD SOME TWISTS OF MY OWN, STARTING WITH BASKETBALL. WOULDN'T IT BE GREAT IF WE COULD ALL SLAM-DUNK LIKE SPUD WEBB?

LET'S LOOK AT FOOTBALL. NOW, THERE'S A FUN-FILLED, BONE-CRUNCHING SPORT. YOU PROBABLY THINK THERE'S NO ROOM FOR IMPROVING THIS POPULAR GAME. WELL, LET ME SHOW YOU MY GENIUS IDEA THAT WILL MAKE THE GAME MORE ENTERTAINING. WE CAN START AT THE PRO LEVEL.

I HATE THIS DOLPHIN SUIT. I WANT TO BE TRADED!

YEAH, WELL HOW WOULD YOU LIKE TO PLAY FOR THE JETS?

ICE HOCKEY IS A WILD GAME. IT'S FAST AND ACTION-PACKED. SOMETIMES THE ACTION GETS SO FAST THAT IT'S HARD TO SEE THE PUCK. I HAVE A WAY TO MAKE IT EASIER FOR THE PLAYERS AND THE SPECTATORS TO FOLLOW WHAT'S HAPPENING ON THE ICE.

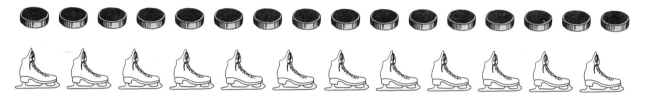

OFF-ROAD SKATEBOARDING!!
AWESOME!
JUST GET SOME OVERSIZED WHEELS WITH SOME BIG TREAD AND...

SAFETY HELMETS WOULD DEFINITELY BE REQUIRED EQUIPMENT.

I'VE NEVER PLAYED GOLF BEFORE, BUT I'VE PLAYED MINIATURE GOLF, AND IT'S GIVEN ME AN IDEA ON HOW TO MAKE **REAL** GOLF TOUGHER.

...17...

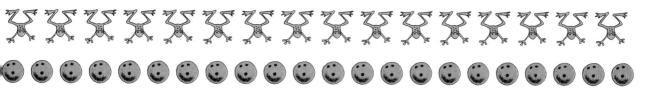

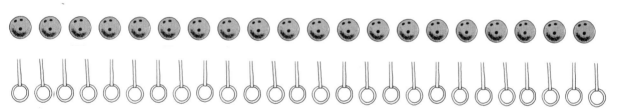

PLAY THE GAME WITH FIVE BALLS AT THE SAME TIME! THERE WOULD BE ACTION ALL OVER THE FIELD.